Baseball Basics
A Quick Guide to America's Favorite Pastime
Deb Witherell

Copyright © 2024 by Deb Witherell

ISBN 978-1-943891-00-9

All rights reserved.

No portion of this book may be reproduced in any form without written permission from the publisher or author, except as permitted by U.S. copyright law.

This publication is designed to provide accurate and authoritative information in regard to the subject matter covered. While the publisher and author have used their best efforts in preparing this book, they make no representations or warranties with respect to the accuracy or completeness of the contents of this book.

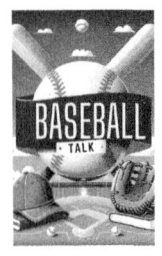

Get your free copy of Baseball Talk: 75 Baseball Terms for Fans of America's Favorite Pastime

https://dl.bookfunnel.com/em8j2rl88k

Contents

1. The Basics of Baseball — 1
2. Understanding the Gameplay — 5
3. Essential Baseball Terms — 8
4. The Role of Strategy in Baseball — 12
5. History and Significance — 15
6. Following a Baseball Game — 18
7. The Major League Baseball (MLB) Universe — 22
8. Join the Baseball Community — 28
9. Advanced Topics in Baseball — 32
10. The Enduring Magic of Baseball — 36
11. Appendix and Resources – Your Toolbox for Baseball Brilliance — 39
12. Wrapping Up the Ballgame – Final Thoughts on Our Baseball Journey — 42
13. Your Free Gift — 45

References — 46

Reviews, Please — 47

Chapter 1
The Basics of Baseball

Baseball: More Than Just a Game

Baseball isn't just a sport; it's a rich history, full of legends, heartbreaks, and triumphant moments. Picture it as a grand drama where the field is the stage, the players are the actors, and every game writes a new story.

The Field: Where Magic Happens

Imagine a diamond, a dusty, grassy one with four bases laid out in a square pattern. In the center of this diamond is a mound, where the pitcher stands, ruling their tiny hill like a king (or queen!). The rest of the players take their places, each guarding their own piece of the realm. The baseball diamond looks like this:

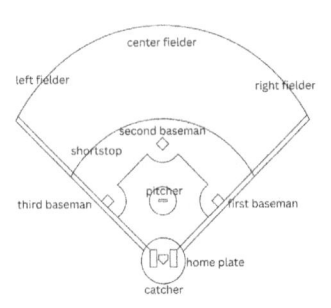

[Diagram of a baseball field showing positions: center fielder, left fielder, right fielder, second baseman, shortstop, third baseman, pitcher, first baseman, home plate, catcher]

The Players: The Knights of the Realm

Each team, when it's their opponent's turn to bat, has nine players on the field at one time, each with a specific role. There are pitchers, catchers, infielders (those guarding the bases), and outfielders (the ones chilling in the grassy part, ready to spring into action). They all have one goal, to outsmart and outplay the other team and prevent them from scoring runs.

When it's their team's turn to bat, each player comes to home plate to face the opposing pitcher. Every at-bat is a game of cat and mouse, strategy, guessing and skill. Which pitch will the pitcher throw? Will the batter swing or let it pass into the catcher's glove? Will the umpire call a ball or a strike? The team at bat scores as many runs as possible before they make three outs.

The Game: A Tale of Innings

Baseball is played in 'innings.' Think of an inning as a chapter in a book. There are nine of these chapters in a standard game. Each inning has two halves: the top (where the visiting team is up at bat and tries to score) and the bottom (where the home team takes its turn). Both teams are focused on scoring more runs than the other team by the end of the game.

In the middle of the seventh inning, there's the 'seventh inning stretch,' where fans stand up, stretch, and walk around. Some sing "God Bless America" or "Take Me out to the Ball Game" too. How long will the game last? Nobody knows. It's not like football or basketball, where fans and players know that, after a certain amount of time passes, the game is over. In baseball, it's over when it's over.

Runs: The Currency of Victory

How do they score these runs? Simple (sort of). A player hits the ball thrown by the pitcher and runs around the bases, from first to second to third to home. Touch all four bases in order, and they've got a run. But, of course, the other team will try their best to stop the runner, which is when things get interesting, and sometimes exciting.

Outs: Avoid Them Like Spoilers

Each team wants to avoid something called 'outs.' Think of outs as plot twists that can either be a bummer or a blessing, depending on which side you're on. Three outs, and your team's turn to bat is over. Then, it's the other team's turn to swing and dash. Sometimes it takes a while to get three outs, and other times they happen in a flash.

The Thrill of the Game

What makes baseball thrilling is the blend of strategy, skill, and a bit of good old-fashioned luck. There's anticipation, guessing what will happen next, and then being totally surprised. It's a chess match, a dance, and a sprint, all rolled into one.

Those are the very basics of baseball. As we dive deeper into the following chapters, you'll discover why millions around the world can't get enough of this sport. It's a game that can be as relaxing as a lazy Sunday afternoon but as gripping as your favorite thriller. Welcome to baseball. Let the fun begin!

Chapter 2
Understanding the Gameplay

The sun is shining, the crowd is buzzing, and the smell of hot dogs and garlic fries fills the air. We're ready to watch the game unfold.

Pitchers: The Wizards of the Mound

The pitcher is the maestro of the mound. They're a blend of power, strategy, and a hint of magic. They hurl the ball towards the batter with one goal: prevent them from hitting it. It's important to throw hard and be unpredictable. Fastballs, curveballs, sliders, these are the spells in their arsenal.

Batters: Swingers of Destiny

Now, meet the batter. They stand at home plate wielding their bat like a knight with a sword, ready to battle the pitcher's sorcery. Their mission? Hit that ball as hard and as strategically as they can. A good batter needs the reflexes of a cat and the patience of a saint. When they connect with the ball and drive it over the outfield wall, over 300 feet away, it's like fireworks!

The Dance of Hits and Runs

What happens when the batter hits the ball? It's time to run! If they whack the ball out of the park (a home run), they can casually trot around the bases. But if the ball stays in play (on the field), it's a mad dash to get as far as they can before the other team recovers the ball and throws it back into the infield. It's part sprint, part game of tag.

Fielders: The Unsung Heroes

Don't forget about the fielders. These guys are the knights in shining armor when they're on defense. They leap, dive, and sprint to catch the ball and get the batters out. Whether it's the shortstop leaping to catch a line drive or the outfielder making a dramatic catch at the fence, these players can make or break a game with spectacular plays.

Three Strikes and You're... Out!

There are a few ways outs can happen: three strikes and you're out, hit the ball in the air and it's caught? Out. Try to get to a base and get tagged before you get there? Also out.

Innings: The Chapters of the Game

Remember the innings? Each team gets to bat in the top or bottom halves, trying to score as many runs as they can. After nine innings, the team with more runs wins. But if the score is tied, brace yourself for extra innings. You're getting free baseball! You'll know the game is over in extra innings when one team scores a run in an inning (maybe the tenth or eleventh) and the other team doesn't score. Two games in modern Major League history have lasted 25 innings!

The Strategy and The Thrill

What's mesmerizing about baseball is the blend of strategy, skill, and sometimes, sheer luck. It's a thinking person's game, but with enough sudden twists to keep your heart racing. Every pitch, every swing, every catch is a story in itself, unfolding in real-time.

That's the roller coaster ride of baseball gameplay. It's fast, it's slow, it's strategic, and above all, it's downright fun.

In the next chapter we'll decode some of the game's secret language.

Chapter 3
Essential Baseball Terms

Welcome to the secret society of baseball speak! There's no secret handshake, but there is a whole lot of quirky lingo that, once you understand and use it, can make you sound like a real pro.

"Batter Up!" – The Call to Adventure

When you hear this, it's game time! The batter heads to the plate, ready to face the pitcher. It's the starting bell of a mini-drama that could end with anything from a strikeout to a home run.

Strikeout – The Swing and a Miss

Three strikes and you're out! A 'strike' can be a swing and miss at whatever the pitcher throws, or a ball zooming into the 'strike zone' (an imaginary box) without the batter swinging. A strikeout? That's when the pitcher totally outsmarts the batter with three strikes. Tough luck for the batter. Now he must take a seat in his team's dugout and wait for his next turn at bat.

No Hitter- The Pitcher's Dream

Can a team play for nine innings and get no hits? Yes, it's possible but not likely. The opposing pitchers must be very good, or very lucky.

Full Count- What's Next?

When there's a 'full count' on a batter, he has three balls and two strikes. One more ball and he walks to first base. One more strike and he's out. Or he could get a hit. Oh, the suspense!

Home Run – The Crowd Goes Wild!

The batter smacks the ball out of the park and gets to take a leisurely victory lap around the bases. High fives all around! The team scores a run. If there are more runners on base, those runners score too. Outfielders will do whatever they can to grab the ball before it's gone. They might climb the outfield wall or make a spectacular jump to save a run and end up with the ball in their glove. The runner may be halfway around the bases before he realizes he's not a hero, he's out.

Grand Slam – Party at the Plate

This is the home run's big sibling. Picture this: the bases are loaded (meaning there's a runner on every base), and the batter hits a home run. All the base runners, plus the batter, run around the bases and score, one run for each runner. That's four runs in one swing. Talk about a game changer!

Double Play – Two for the Price of One

It's baseball's version of a two-for-one deal. The fielding team gets two outs in one play. The batter hits the ball, and two runners are called out. This bit of bad luck for the hitter happens in a variety of ways. The fielder's speed, skill, and agility make the difference.

Bullpen – Where the Pitchers Chill

As you might expect, no bulls are in the bullpen. It's where relief pitchers (who take over for the starting pitcher part way through the game) warm up before they step into the game. Think of it as the backstage area for pitchers.

Error – Oops!

Even baseball players have 'oops' moments. An error is when a fielder bungles a play they usually would make. They might drop a fly ball or make a wild throw that allows a base runner to advance.

Walk – A Free Stroll to First Base

When the pitcher throws four balls outside the strike zone, the batter gets to walk to first base without having to swing the bat.

RBI – Run Batted In

An RBI happens when a batter hits the ball and a runner scores as a result. Yay for teamwork!

The Mound – The Pitcher's Throne

This is where the pitcher stands. It's a slightly raised area in the center of the diamond. The mound is the pitcher's domain, their turf, the spot where they conjure their pitching magic.

Dugout – The Team's Hangout

Those bench areas along the sidelines? That's the dugout, the team's headquarters, where players sit when they're not on the field. It's a prime spot for gum-chewing and sunflower-seed-spitting. And sometimes heckling the umpire when the players disagree with his call.

Next up, we'll delve into the chess-like strategies of baseball.

Chapter 4
The Role of Strategy in Baseball

If you thought this game was just about throwing, hitting, and running, prepare to be amazed. Baseball is a giant, grassy game of chess, full of strategies, mind games, and crafty maneuvers.

The Art of Pitching: It's Not Just Throw and Go

Think of the pitcher as a crafty wizard. They're not just hurling the ball; they're plotting. Fastballs, curveballs, sliders, each pitch is a chess move. The goal? Outwit the batter and keep them guessing. It's a high-speed duel, and brains are just as important as brawn.

Batting Strategy: More Than Just Swinging

Batters don't just swing willy-nilly. They study the pitcher, looking for patterns, weaknesses. Should they aim for a power hit or just try to get on base? It's about picking their battles and sometimes being patient enough to draw a walk.

Fielding Formations: The Defensive Dance

Fielders are constantly shifting, adjusting their positions based on the batter's tendencies and the game situation. It's a dance choreographed by the manager and the players, full of anticipation and quick moves. One step left or right could be the difference between an out and a run.

The Steal: A Dash of Daring

A base stealer is like a stealthy ninja. The runner on base watches the pitcher like a hawk. Then, in a heartbeat, they're off, sprinting towards the next base, trying to get there before the ball does. It's risky, it's bold, and oh boy, is it thrilling to watch!

Bunting: Small Ball, Big Impact

Bunting is when the batter lightly taps the ball, making it roll slowly. It sounds easy, but it's a strategic gem. Used to advance runners or surprise the defense, a well-placed bunt can be a game-changer. It's like playing subtle, strategic pool with a baseball bat.

The Manager's Role: The Puppet Master

The manager doesn't play on the field, but they're the grand strategist. They decide when to switch pitchers, where to position players, and when to take risks. They're the masterminds, analyzing every detail and making calls that can turn the game on its head.

The Sign Language of Baseball

Watch the players and coaches, and you'll see a flurry of signals and signs. Touching the cap, wiping the nose, tugging an ear, it's a secret code, communicating strategies without saying a word, like spies exchanging covert messages in a thriller movie.

Playing the Matchups: Chess with People

Baseball loves its statistics, and managers use them to play the matchups. They'll switch pitchers or batters based on who's up to bat or on the mound, playing the odds for the best outcome. It's a numbers game, and a little math can go a long way.

This the strategic soul of baseball. It's a game of intellect, intuition, and sometimes, sheer gut feeling.

Next we'll explore the sport's rich history and legendary moments.

Chapter 5
History and Significance

Baseball is a saga etched in the annals of time, peppered with legends, epic moments, and a few scandals to spice things up. Sit back, relax, and let's rewind the clock to where it all began.

The Origins: A Mysterious Beginning

The true origin of baseball is a bit like a 'who-dun-it' mystery. Some say it evolved from the British game of rounders, while others claim it's as American as apple pie. But one thing's for sure, by the late 19th century, baseball was America's pastime.

Babe Ruth: The Sultan of Swat

No history of baseball is complete without Babe Ruth. This guy was like the Elvis of baseball, a larger-than-life character with a bat that launched home runs like rockets. He changed the game, turned it into a spectacle, and became a legend in the process.

Breaking Barriers: Jackie Robinson's Triumph

In 1947, Jackie Robinson did more than play baseball. He smashed through racial barriers. As the first African American to play in Major League Baseball in the modern era, he faced hostility, prejudice, and immense pressure with dignity and talent. He didn't just play the game; he changed it forever.

The Miracle Mets: Underdogs Write History

In 1969, enter the New York Mets. They were the lovable underdogs, a team nobody expected much from. But in a twist fit for a Hollywood script, they clinched the World Series, leaving the baseball world in awe. It was a reminder that in baseball, anything's possible.

The Home Run Chase: McGwire and Sosa's Summer Saga

Fast forward to 1998 – Mark McGwire and Sammy Sosa were locked in a home run race for the ages, chasing Roger Maris's long-standing record of 61 home runs in one season. It was a summer-long thriller, capturing the nation's imagination. It was dramatic, controversial, and unforgettable. McGwire ended the season with 70 home runs, while Sammy Sosa whacked 66 out of the park.

Steroids Scandal: A Shadow Over the Game

Not all history is heroic, though. The late '90s and early 2000's saw a steroid scandal that rocked the baseball world. Big names were involved, records were tainted, and baseball's integrity took a hit. It was a tough time, but it led to stricter policies and a new era of transparency.

The Red Sox Break the Curse
2004 – a year of redemption for the Boston Red Sox and their fans. After an 86-year drought, they finally won the World Series, breaking the infamous 'Curse of the Bambino'. It was a fairy-tale ending, a mix of relief and euphoria, and a testament to the enduring spirit of baseball fans.

The Global Game: Baseball Around the World
Today, baseball is more than an American pastime. It's played all over the world, from the Dominican Republic to Japan, where it's a cultural phenomenon. The World Baseball Classic showcases this global love affair, uniting countries in their shared passion for the game.

This is a sampling of baseball's rich, diverse, and sometimes controversial history. It's a tapestry woven with threads of triumph, adversity, and resilience.

Up next, we'll delve into the art of following a baseball game. Whether you're a rookie or a seasoned fan, there's always something new to learn in the ever-evolving world of baseball.

Chapter 6
Following a Baseball Game

Here in the big leagues of fandom, the popcorn's hot, the cheers are loud, and every game is an adventure! Whether you're watching from the couch or the bleachers, there's an art to enjoying a baseball game. Grab your fielder's glove and let's dive into the fantastic world of following baseball.

The Scoreboard – Your Game Day Map

First up, the scoreboard. This is more than a bunch of numbers and names; it's your treasure map to understanding the game. It tells you the score, the inning, the count (balls and strikes), and who's up to bat. At first glance, it might look like a math problem, but once you crack the code, you're in the know.

At the Stadium – Soak in the Atmosphere
If you're lucky enough to be at the game, soak it all in. The roar of the crowd, the smell of hotdogs, the seventh-inning stretch, it's an experience that's more than just watching a game; it's feeling it. Tip: always keep an eye on the field. You don't want to miss a home run while you're sharing your nachos!

Watching on TV – The Comfort of Home
Watching on TV has its perks. You get replays, commentary, and the best seat in the house: your couch. The commentators are like your personal game-day guides, offering insights, stats, great baseball stories and sometimes, a good chuckle.

Understanding the Commentary – Speak Baseball
Baseball commentary is an art form. They'll throw terms like 'double play', 'RBI', and 'ERA' at you. Don't fret; remember Chapter 3? You've got a great start in understanding baseball-ese.

The In-Game Experience – Beyond the Play
Be ready for more than just the play on the field. There's the mascot antics, fan contests, and sing-alongs. It's a carnival wrapped around a sports event. It's part of what makes baseball, well, baseball.

Understanding the Strategy – Think Like a Manager

As you watch more games, start thinking like a manager. Would you have called for a bunt there? Should that pitcher be replaced? It's a game within a game, and it deepens your appreciation for the sport.

The Role of Umpires – More Than Just Calling Balls and Strikes

The umpires are the sheriffs of baseball town. There are four umpires in a major league game: one behind home plate (calling balls and strikes), and one near each of the other bases. They call balls, strikes, outs, and keep the game in order. They might not always be popular (especially if they make a call against your team), but they're a crucial part of the game. They can toss players, coaches and managers out of the game if things get out of order. You can recognize umpires because they aren't wearing the uniforms of either team. They usually wear blue, black, or grey shirts and pants and a cap with the major league logo.

Keeping Score – Old-School Cool

Try keeping score. It's an ancient fan tradition, where you jot down every play in a special scorebook. It's a symbolic language that creates a historical document of the game, and it's oddly satisfying.

The Official Scorer- Was it a Hit or an Error?

Who decides? There's an official scorer watching every play at every game. They're appointed by the league to keep track of everything and make decisions about plays, according to the many rules of Major League Baseball (MLB). The 2023 MLB official rule book has 192 pages! Most official scorers are seasoned baseball writers, broadcasters, or former players. They've scored games at the minor league level and have a thorough understanding of the rules of the game.

The Social Side – Join the Community

Baseball is a social sport. Chat with the fans around you, join a fan club, engage in online forums. Share your highs, your lows and your 'what was that umpire thinking?' moments. It's all part of being in the baseball family.

Whether you're at the game or watching from afar, each experience is unique, exciting, and full of memories in the making.

Coming up, get ready to meet the stars, the teams, and the traditions that make Major League Baseball a global phenomenon.

Chapter 7
The Major League Baseball (MLB) Universe

Welcome to 'The Show,' the main event, the grand stage of baseball: Major League Baseball (MLB)! This is where legends are born, heroes are made, and hot dogs taste better than anywhere else. Let's take a VIP tour of the MLB universe, where every pitch, hit, and catch is epic.

MLB 101: The Basics

The MLB is the Hollywood of baseball, featuring 30 teams split into two leagues: the American League (AL) and the National League (NL). Each league has its own quirks and traditions.

The Teams: From Coast to Coast

From the New York Yankees to the Los Angeles Dodgers, each team has its own story, fan base, and unique vibe. Some are steeped in history, while others are newer kids on the block. Pick a team, wear their colors, and join a tribe that spans generations.

Divisions: How They're Organized

MLB has two leagues: American and National. Each league is divided into three divisions: East, Central and West. Five teams make up each division. Here they are:

American League:
East: Toronto Blue Jays, Boston Red Sox, New York Yankees, Baltimore Orioles, and Tampa Rays
Central: Minnesota Twins, Chicago White Sox, Cleveland Guardians, Kansas City Royals, and Detroit Tigers
West: Oakland Athletics, Los Angeles Angels, Seattle Mariners, Houston Astros, and Texas Rangers
National League:
East: New York Mets, Washington Nationals, Florida Marlins, Philadelphia Phillies, and Atlanta Braves
Central: Chicago Cubs, St. Louis Cardinals, Pittsburgh Pirates, Milwaukee Brewers, and Cincinnati Reds
West: Los Angeles Dodgers, San Diego Padres, San Francisco Giants, Arizona Diamondbacks, and Colorado Rockies

Spring Training: Ready, Set Go!

In February and March, major league teams gather in Florida (grapefruit league) and Arizona (cactus league) to tune up for the regular season. They meet their new teammates and build strength and skill to get ready for Opening Day. Minor leaguers are invited too, to try to earn a spot on the team. Then teams head for their first regular season game, either as the home team or the visitors, in a major league stadium.

Opening Day: At Last!

Opening Day of the season brings excitement from coast to coast. Fans wait all winter for this! Red, white, and blue bunting hangs from the upper decks. Aromas of popcorn and hot dogs fill the air. Fans get a look at new players, greet their favorites, and rekindle dreams of postseason victories and World Series rings.

Interleague Play: More Variety

During the season, teams from the American and National league play against each other. Fans get a chance to see players they might not know and watch different styles of play.

The Regular Season: A Marathon, Not a Sprint

The MLB season is a marathon, running from April to October, with each team playing a whopping 162 games. That's a total of 4,860 games! It's a test of endurance, skill, and strategy. The goal? Rack up enough wins to make it to the postseason.

The Postseason: Where Legends Are Made
Now the intensity skyrockets. The best teams from each league battle it out in the playoffs, culminating in the World Series, a best-of-seven showdown that crowns the champion. It's dramatic, it's nail-biting, and it's where baseball immortality is up for grabs. And World Series rings, too!

The All-Star Game: The Stars Align
Midway through the season comes the All-Star Game, where the best players from each league face off in a star-studded exhibition game between the American League and the National League. It's every fan's dream. Fans get to vote for their favorite players and help decide who will represent their team in this battle of the bats and gloves.

Traditions and Rivalries: The Heart and Soul of MLB
Baseball is rich in traditions and heated rivalries. From the singing of "Take Me Out to the Ball Game" in the seventh inning stretch, to the legendary rivalry between the Boston Red Sox and the New York Yankees, these traditions add flavor and fervor to the game.

Legends of the Game: Heroes of the Diamond
MLB has been home to some of the greatest athletes in sports history: Babe Ruth, Ted Williams, Willie Mays, Hank Aaron, and many more. Their stories are the stuff of legend. Fans get to witness history in the making when one of their heroes steps up to the plate or robs a home run with a spectacular jump at the center field wall.

The World Series: The Ultimate Baseball Showdown
The World Series is the climax of the MLB season. It's where dreams are fulfilled or crushed, where heroes rise, and unforgettable

moments are etched in history. Winning the World Series is the ultimate glory in baseball.

The Hall of Fame: Heroes of Cooperstown

Every July, in the small village (population about 2,000) of Cooperstown, New York, hundreds of baseball fans arrive to honor new inductees at the Baseball Hall of Fame. These players are the superstars of baseball. They join the almost 300 players, managers, owners, and others who have starred in the game throughout history. It's the crowning glory that players dream about long before they put on a major league uniform.

Minor Leagues and Beyond: The Grassroots

The MLB is just the tip of the iceberg. There's a whole world of little league, minor league, college, and international baseball, each with its own charms and stars-in-the-making. It's a reminder that baseball thrives at all levels, all around the world. Players spend years working their way up through the levels, honing their skills and staying ready for that call that will send them to 'The Show.'

The Global Impact: Baseball Around the World

Baseball has gone global, with MLB games played in countries like Japan and Mexico, and international players becoming household names in the U.S. It's a game that speaks a universal language of excitement, passion, and community. Every 3 to 4 years, beginning in 2006, teams from everywhere have come together to represent their countries and compete in the World Baseball Classic.

From its legendary teams to its rich traditions, the MLB is more than a league; it's a cultural phenomenon.

In the next chapter, we'll explore how to engage with the baseball community, from fan clubs to fantasy leagues.

Chapter 8
Join the Baseball Community

The baseball community is a vibrant, buzzing world. It's a family, a social network, where you can high-five strangers like they're old pals.

Join the Fan Club – Where Passion Meets People

Every team has its fan club, and these are not just any clubs. They're your ticket to a community of like-minded, baseball-crazy folks. Join up, and you'll find yourself swapping stories, attending exclusive events, and maybe even getting some sweet team mementos.

Social Media – The Digital Dugout

Follow your team on social media. It's a digital dugout, where you get real-time updates, behind-the-scenes glimpses, and a chance to interact with fellow fans (and sometimes even the players). Plus, it's the go-to place for epic memes and gifs.

Fantasy Baseball – Be the Manager

Ever dreamed of managing your own baseball team? Fantasy baseball turns that dream into a virtual reality. Draft your players, set your lineup, and compete with friends (or strangers) in a stats-driven baseball bonanza. It's addictive, fun, and a whole new way to engage with the game.

Ballpark Visits – The Ultimate Fan Experience

There's nothing like watching a game live at the ballpark. It's an immersive experience that combines sports, entertainment, and community. Tour different stadiums, soak in the unique atmospheres, and don't forget to sample some ballpark-exclusive snacks.

Collectibles – Treasure Hunting for Fans

Baseball cards, autographed balls, vintage jerseys – collecting memorabilia is a hobby that can turn you into a baseball historian and treasure hunter rolled into one. It's a tangible way to connect with the game's history and your favorite players.

Engaging in Forums and Blogs – The Think Tank

Online forums and baseball blogs are where the armchair managers, stats gurus, and passionate fans collide in a symphony of opinions, analyses, and heated debates. Join in, share your thoughts, and maybe learn a thing or two from other enthusiasts.

Baseball Video Games – Swing Virtually

Want to hit a home run off a major league pitcher without leaving your couch? Baseball video games let you live out your diamond dreams digitally. It's a fun way to understand the nuances of the game and, of course, to brag about your virtual batting average.

Community Events and Charity Work – Give Back with Baseball

Baseball is about community, and many teams and fan groups organize charity events and community projects. Participate in these, and you're not just supporting a good cause, you're living the true spirit of the game.

Watching Parties and Meetups – Share the Excitement

Nothing beats watching a game with a group of fans. Organize or join a watching party, and you'll find the cheers (and groans) twice as loud and the game three times as fun. It's a great way to make friends and immerse yourself in the fan culture.

From the roar of the stadium to the buzz of online communities, being a baseball fan is about being part of something bigger than yourself.

Next, we'll explore some advanced aspects of baseball, when you're ready to deepen your understanding of the game.

Chapter 9
Advanced Topics in Baseball

This is the big brain section, where we dive into the deeper end of the baseball pool. This chapter is for those of you who've got the basics down and are ready for the more intricate, mind-bending aspects of baseball. Put on your thinking caps and let's unravel the mysteries of advanced baseball.

Sabermetrics: The Science of Baseball

In this part of the baseball world, sabermetrics, baseball meets mathematics, statistics, and a dash of wizardry. Sabermetrics is all about analyzing baseball through hardcore stats to make better decisions on player performance, game strategies, and team composition. It's being a baseball detective and finding clues hidden in numbers.

The Physics of Pitching

Ever wonder how a pitcher throws a curveball that seems to defy gravity? It's all physics! The way a pitcher grips the ball, the spin they put on it, and the air resistance all contribute to those mind-bending pitches. Understanding the physics of pitching is like unlocking the secrets of a baseball magician's handbook.

Advanced Scouting and Player Analysis

Scouting in baseball isn't just watching players and taking notes. It's an intricate process involving player stats, historical performance, injury history, and even psychological factors. Advanced scouting is like putting together a giant, living jigsaw puzzle where every piece is a player.

The Art of Managing a Bullpen

Managing a bullpen is like being a chess master. A manager must know when to pull a pitcher out of the game, whom to bring in as relief, and how to outmaneuver the opposing team's batting lineup. It's a high-stakes game of strategy, foresight, and guts.

The Mental Game: Psychology in Baseball

Baseball is as much a mental game as it is physical. Coping with pressure, maintaining focus, and the psychological duel between pitcher and batter are critical for success. It's a mental marathon, where the strongest minds often lead to the most remarkable plays.

The Economics of Baseball

Baseball isn't just a sport; it's big business. Understanding the economics of baseball, from player contracts and salary caps to revenue sharing and media rights, is like pulling back the curtain on how the baseball world really spins.

Advanced Statistics: Beyond the Basics

Ready to level up your stats game? WAR (Wins Above Replacement), BABIP (Batting Average on Balls in Play), and FIP (Fielding Independent Pitching) are just a few of the advanced stats that give a deeper insight into the game's complexities. It's a numbers feast for the baseball-hungry mind.

The Evolution of Training and Health

Gone are the days of just 'hit and throw.' Modern training techniques, nutrition, injury prevention, and recovery methods are revolutionizing how players train and maintain their health. It's a blend of science, technology, and old-fashioned sweat. Major league teams hire strength and conditioning coaches to help players make the most of their physical skills.

Baseball and Technology: The Digital Revolution

From instant replays to Artificial Intelligence-powered analytics, technology is changing the face of baseball. It's enhancing how games are played, watched, and analyzed. This digital revolution is adding a turbo boost to the classic game of baseball. In 2022, Major League Baseball approved the use of Pitch Com, an electronic device catchers use to tell pitchers what kind of pitch to throw and where to throw it. Gone are the days of catchers squatting behind home plate, flashing signs to the pitcher. It turns out that those signs were too easy for the other team to steal. Enter Pitch Com, the electronic solution.

Whether you're a stats geek, a physics enthusiast, or just curious about the inner workings of the game, baseball has layers of complexity that can keep you fascinated for a lifetime.

Chapter 10
The Enduring Magic of Baseball

And here we are, at the final inning of our baseball journey. We've laughed, we've learned, and maybe we've even shed a tear or two (especially if your team was on the losing end of a no-hitter). Let's take a moment to reflect on the enduring magic of baseball and why this isn't just a game, but a slice of life.

Baseball: A Mirror of Life

Baseball is a metaphor for life. It's about teamwork and individuality, triumphs and failures, strategy, and spontaneity. It teaches resilience, patience, and the importance of seizing opportunities. Like life, it's unpredictable, challenging, and can be oh-so-rewarding.

The Cultural Impact: Beyond the Field

From literature to movies, fashion to folklore, baseball has permeated every aspect of culture. It's inspired artists, writers, and filmmakers, shaping our collective consciousness. Baseball terms like 'out of left field' and 'hit a home run' have even found their way into our everyday language.

The Global Game: Uniting the World

What started as an American pastime has become a global phenomenon. Baseball bridges cultures, bringing people together from Japan to the Dominican Republic, from Canada to South Korea. It's a universal language of excitement and passion, a shared experience that knows no borders.

The Community: A Family of Fans

Baseball's true heart lies in its community, the fans. From little league stands to major league stadiums, it's about the shared experiences, the communal cheers, and even the collective groans. It's where lifelong friendships are forged, and generations bond over the crack of a bat.

The Timeless Appeal: A Game for All Ages

Baseball is timeless. It's as enchanting for a wide-eyed kid experiencing their first game as it is for the seasoned fan who's seen a thousand. It's a thread that runs through generations, a constant in a world of change.

The Future of Baseball: Evolving and Enduring

Baseball continues to evolve with technology, new rules, and emerging global talent. But at its core, it remains the same game that captured hearts over a century ago, a game of strategy, skill, and a little bit of magic.

The Personal Journey: Your Baseball Story

Remember that baseball is your story, too. Whether you're a player, a fan, a statistician, or just a casual observer, you're part of the grand tapestry that is baseball. Cherish your memories, your experiences, and your connection to this incredible game.

In baseball, as in life, there's always more to learn, more to experience, and more to love. Keep watching, keep cheering, and keep loving the game. Here's to baseball, the sport, the legend, the endless source of joy and wonder.

Chapter 11
Appendix and Resources — Your Toolbox for Baseball Brilliance

As we round third and head for home in our baseball odyssey, let's not forget that every great player, manager, or fan needs a trusty toolkit. Consider this chapter your utility belt, packed with resources, references, and little nuggets of knowledge to keep your baseball game strong and your fan flames burning bright!

Further Reading: Books to Feed Your Baseball Brain

Want to dive deeper? There's a library's worth of fantastic baseball books out there. From the classic *Ball Four* by Jim Bouton to *Moneyball* by Michael Lewis, these books offer insights, stories, and a behind-the-scenes look at the game we love.

Must-Watch Movies: Baseball on the Big Screen

Baseball and movies are like peanuts and Cracker Jacks, a perfect pairing. Classics like 'Field of Dreams', 'The Sandlot', and 'Bull Durham' capture the spirit, nostalgia, and romance of the game. Pop some corn and enjoy a baseball movie night!

Documentaries: The Real-Life Drama of Baseball

For the factual fanatics among us, documentaries like 'Ken Burns' Baseball' and 'The Tenth Inning' are gold mines. They delve into the history, the legends, and the cultural impact of baseball, bringing the real-life drama of the game to your screen.

Online Resources: The Digital Diamond

The internet is your friend when it comes to staying updated and informed. Websites like MLB.com, Baseball-Reference.com, and FanGraphs offer a wealth of stats, player bios, and up-to-the-minute news. It's like having a baseball encyclopedia at your fingertips.

Podcasts and Radio Shows: Baseball for Your Ears

Whether you're commuting or chilling, baseball podcasts and radio shows can be great companions. Check out shows like 'Effectively Wild' or 'The Ringer MLB Show' for insightful analysis, player interviews, and all the latest baseball chatter.

Social Media Accounts to Follow: Your Daily Dose of Baseball

From official team accounts to player profiles and fan pages, social media is bustling with baseball content. Follow your favorites for a mix of updates, insights, and a healthy dose of humor.

Apps for the Avid Fan: Baseball at Your Fingertips

Want to track games, scores, and stats on the go? Apps like MLB At Bat and ESPN are great for keeping you in the loop. They're like having a tiny baseball butler in your pocket.

Forums and Fan Groups: Join the Conversation

Online forums and fan groups are fantastic for connecting with fellow baseball enthusiasts. Reddit's r/baseball, team-specific forums, and Facebook groups are bustling hubs where you can debate, discuss, and delve into everything baseball.

Local Leagues and Community Clubs: Get into the Game

And finally, don't forget to support your local baseball scene. Whether it's a minor league team, a college squad, or a community club, there's something special about cheering for the home team and being part of the grassroots game.

There's an endless supply of baseball goodness to explore. In baseball, as in life, the learning never stops, and the fun never fades. Keep swinging, keep dreaming, and keep enjoying the magic of baseball!

Chapter 12
Wrapping Up the Ballgame – Final Thoughts on Our Baseball Journey

We've reached the bottom of the ninth in our **Baseball Basics** adventure. It's been a fun ride through the ins and outs, the ups and downs, and the home runs and strikeouts of this incredible game. Before we call it a game, let's have a quick seventh-inning stretch and reflect on what we've covered and the lasting joy of baseball.

The Love of the Game: More Than Just Numbers and Rules

Remember, baseball is more than just stats, players, and innings. It's a feeling. It's the thrill of a close play at home plate, the suspense of a full count, and the camaraderie of cheering with thousands of fans. It's a sport that captures the heart and the imagination.

A Journey Through Baseball: From Rookies to Regulars

We started as rookies, but look at us now! We've journeyed through the basics, the lingo, the strategies, and the heart-pounding action of the game. We've relived historic moments, embraced the fandom, and even peeked into the brainy side of baseball.

Baseball as a Universal Language: Connecting Us All

One of the beautiful things about baseball is how it connects us. Young or old, rookie or veteran, there's a place for everyone in the world of baseball. It's a universal language that speaks of passion, perseverance, and the pursuit of greatness.

Your Baseball Story: Continuing the Adventure

Now, it's your turn. Your baseball story is just beginning. Go to games, join fan clubs, debate with friends, and maybe even start playing yourself. There's no right or wrong way to enjoy baseball. It's all about what the game means to you.

The Game Goes On: Baseball's Everlasting Appeal

Baseball, like life, is ever-changing, yet some things remain timeless. The crack of the bat, the cheer of the crowd, and the thrill of the game are eternal. As long as there are sunny afternoons and starry evenings, the game of baseball will continue to captivate and inspire.

A Final Tip of the Cap: Thanks for the Memories

As we close this book, let's tip our caps to the great game of baseball. Thanks for the memories, the lessons, and the joy. Whether you're watching from the bleachers or from your living room, the magic of baseball is always just a pitch away.

Keep the Ball Rolling: Never Stop Learning and Loving the Game

The game isn't over; it's just the beginning. Keep learning, keep exploring, and most importantly, keep loving the game. Baseball is a journey with no end, a story that's always unfolding, a game that's forever young.

And with that, we step off the diamond and back into the world, with a newfound appreciation and love for baseball. Remember, in the great ballpark of life, every day is a chance to play ball, to be a part of something bigger, and to enjoy the simple beauty of a game that's been loved for generations.

Thanks for joining me on this journey through **Baseball Basics**. Now, go out there and spread the baseball love. Play ball!

Chapter 13
Your Free Gift

GET YOUR FREE COPY OF

Baseball Talk: 75 Baseball Terms for Fans of America's Favorite Pastime

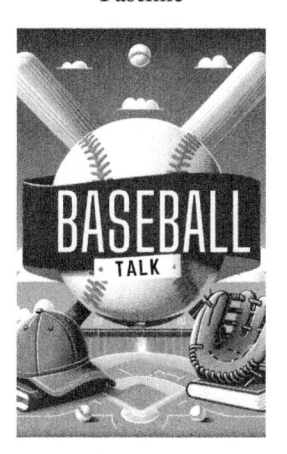

Get your free copy of **Baseball Talk: 75 Baseball Terms for Fans of America's Favorite Pastime** at:

https://dl.bookfunnel.com/em8j2rl88k

References

https://mlb.com

https://www.baseball-reference.com

https://www.ump-attire.com

https://www.baseballrulesacademy.com

Reviews, Please

If you liked **Baseball Basics**, would you leave a review on the Baseball Basics Amazon page? Thanks!

Printed in Great Britain
by Amazon